AMAZING MAGIC™

SIMPLE SLEIGHT-OF-HAND

Card and Coin Tricks for the Beginning Magician

Paul Zenon

rosen publishing's
rosen central®

New York

North American edition first published in 2008 by:

The Rosen Publishing Group, Inc.
29 East 21st Street, New York, NY 10010

North American edition copyright © 2008 by The Rosen Publishing Group, Inc.
First published as *Street Magic* in the United Kingdom, copyright © 2005 by Carlton
Books Limited. Text copyright © 2005 by Paul Zenon. Additional end matter copy-
right © 2008 The Rosen Publishing Group, Inc.

North American edition book design: Nelson Sá
North American edition editor: Nicholas Croce
Photography: Karl Adamson (tricks), Rich Hardcastle (remaining images)

Library of Congress Cataloging-in-Publication Data

Zenon, Paul.
Simple sleight-of-hand: card and coin tricks for the beginning magician / Paul Zenon.
   p. cm.—(Amazing magic)
ISBN-13: 978-1-4042-1070-7 ISBN: 1-4042-1757-6 (pbk)
1. Card tricks—Juvenile literature. 2. Coin tricks—Juvenile literature. 3. Magic
tricks—Juvenile literature.
I. Title.
GV1549.Z46 2007
793.8—dc22

2007008385

Manufactured in the United States of America

CONTENTS

INTRODUCTION

Time to learn some magic, so let's start with something easy. The tricks in this book are designed to give you a taste of what it's like to be a magician. They're virtually self-working, so you don't have to worry about carrying out complicated moves—you can devote all your effort to making the routine as entertaining as possible. Learn a couple of them and try them out on your friends. Be warned though: applause and admiration can be addictive!

Ready for something tougher? Tricks with money always go down well and in this book you'll learn some classics. There are hundreds of tricks with coins and the reason is that they're great things to manipulate. They can be palmed, vanished, and produced very easily.

I've described some of the basic building blocks of sleight-of-hand magic in this book. Learn these well and you'll be ready for more advanced tricks with all kinds of objects.

TRICK 1

You had an accident when you were a child. You banged your head when you fell down the stairs, and ever since you've had a kind of heightened intuition—at least, that's what you've been telling your spectators. The accident left you with strange psychic powers and you're now about to demonstrate them.

You take three cups and borrow a small personal object from one of the spectators. While your back is turned, the spectator places it under one of the cups and then moves a couple of them around to further confuse you. However, using your special psychic gift you can turn around and lift the correct cup to reveal the hidden object.

You can use any three cups for this, from your best china to disposable cardboard ones. The only bit of preparation is that one of the cups must be subtly marked so that you can distinguish it from the other two. It can be a slight flaw in the china, a pencil mark, a dent or nail nick in the cardboard. It shouldn't be something glaringly obvious, as shown in the photos, but something tiny that only you will notice. With that in mind, here are the rest of the instructions:

Lay the cups, mouth-down, in a line on the table and note the position of your marked cup. Let's assume it's the middle cup of the three (1). Turn your back and ask one of the spectators to take out some personal object that will fit under the cup. The person can use a ring or lipstick, anything that will fit. Tell the person to place the object secretly under one of the cups. Tell him to confuse matters a little further by switching the positions of the two empty cups. Chances are you'll hear him do this, but ask him to tell you when he is finished anyway. Then turn around to face the cups and the spectators. Extend your hands and rub them together as if generating some kind of static electricity. You aren't; it just looks vaguely mysterious and makes the audience think the way the trick works has something to do with this.

Ask the spectator who loaned the object to identify himself and, as soon as he steps forward, extend one of your hands and touch him. Again, this has absolutely nothing to do with the trick, but it'll make what you do next look more magical.

Keep your hand extended and move it over the cups. Pretend that you're feeling for some kind of psychic vibrations. What you're really doing is looking for your marked cup because the position of that cup will reveal the position of the object. You know that the marked cup started in the middle. If it's still there, you know that the object is underneath it. That's because the spectators were asked to switch the two cups that were not covering the object. If the marked cup is on the right, though, it means the object must be under the cup on the left (2). Conversely, if the marked cup is on the left, then the object must be under the cup on the right (3). Think about it and you'll see

how a marked cup and some simple instructions can reveal the object's position.

Next comes the important phase: revelation. Build it up. Don't just lift the correct cup; that makes it look too easy. Pause a while and stare into their eyes. Look as if you really are picking up psychic vibrations. Keep the spectators in suspense and, finally, say, "It seems to be this one," and lift the correct cup. Do it right, and they will believe that you have extraordinary powers.

NOTES

This trick bears repeating. It's worth adding a few lines of bogus explanation when asking for an object, too: for example, "It doesn't work with anything made of rubber—but metal, plastic, and paper are fine." It takes the audience's mind away from the real method and makes them think that perhaps there really is something special about your mental powers after all. Remember that the marked cup doesn't have to start in the middle. As long as you know the starting position of the marked cup, you can use logic to work out the position of the object. This means that you can let them arrange the cups on the table. The less you touch the cups, the more impressive the trick will be.

TRICK 2

This is a comical trick with a coin and a pen. You say you're going to make the coin disappear. You hit it three times with the pen, but instead of the coin disappearing, the pen does. Where did it go? You turn your head to reveal that it hasn't actually vanished at all—it's tucked behind your ear. When you draw their attention back to the coin, though, this time it really has disappeared.

This trick is all about timing and a widely used principle in magic called misdirection. It works because while the audience is keeping a keen eye on the coin, you're busy sneaking the pen away. Then, when their attention is focused on the pen, you secretly get rid of the coin. That's basically what misdirection is all about: diverting the audience's attention to where you want it rather than where it might naturally be, thereby allowing you to carry out all kinds of sneaky moves.

Take out a coin and place it on your left palm. Say, "Let me show you this—it's not quite ready, but I think I've got the hang of it—it's the vanishing coin trick." You take a pen from your pocket to use as a magic wand (1). You then say, "You just tap the coin three times with the pen and it completely disappears—watch." Stand with your left

side angled slightly toward the audience. Raise your right hand high, bending it at the elbow, and bring the pen down to hit the coin, counting "One." Do the same again, counting "Two." (2)

As you raise the pen a third time, you shove it behind your ear (3) and, without breaking the stride, count "Three," bringing your empty right hand down as if to hit the coin again. Do a comic double-take as you suddenly notice that the pen isn't there anymore (4). "Hang on—I think I got it the wrong way around," you say. "Maybe it's the pen that was supposed to disappear!" Give it a moment for them to register that the pen's gone and then say, "Actually, some of you might have spotted how I did that!" Turn your head around slowly and point out the pen wedged behind your ear (5).

This should get a laugh from the audience, thinking that the whole thing's just a gag rather than an actual trick. That's your misdirection, though: as you remove the pen from behind your ear, your left hand secretly drops the coin into your left pocket, which is covered by your

body. As soon as you've ditched it, your left hand returns to the palm-up position as you turn back around. Hold the left hand as if it's still holding the coin, but with the fingers slightly curled so that the audience can't see that it's not actually there anymore. "But the weird thing is," you say, "when the pen comes back. . . that's when the coin actually goes!" Tap your left fingers with the pen and slowly open them to reveal that the coin has indeed disappeared (6).

NOTES

The method for this trick is very simple, but it's a great quick one if you play it well and it doesn't require any preparation. It takes pratice to get the timing right on the upward swings of the right hand so that when you leave the pen behind your ear, you don't break the rhythm. The reason no one sees the pen go is because their attention is centered exclusively on the coin in your left hand. You've told them that the coin will disappear and they're intent on seeing that happen. It's amazing how people will miss anything that happens outside their own small circle of focus.

TRICK 3

In this trick, you appear to make playing cards cling to the palm of your hand as if they're magnetized.

To do this trick, you need a small amount of stationery adhesive hidden in your right hand. It's pressed against the middle finger and concealed (1). You also need a deck of playing cards. Begin by shuffling your feet on the floor as if building up static electricity. Tell the spectators, "This isn't really magic; it's something most people can do—unless you're wearing rubber soles. It doesn't work with rubber soles." This is a lie, but all part of the psychological buildup. Ask someone to count

off ten playing cards from the deck onto your left palm, which is facing up. Push off the top card on to the right fingers (2).

Press the card against the adhesive and then hold the right hand out flat, palm-upward. It looks as if the card is simply lying on the open hand. Shuffle one of your feet against the floor as if trying to build up a little more static. This is the kind of bizarre behavior that will make them think it's genuine. Start to slide the ten cards, one at a time, between that first card and your hand in a fairly even but random-looking fashion around it (3).

Continue sliding cards into position until they're all used up (4). You now have a bunch of cards balanced on your hand. Place your left hand on top of the right, sandwiching all the cards. Extend your arms and, still holding the cards between your hands, slowly turn the cards upside down (5). "OK, let's try it," you say and slowly take your left hand away—all the cards appear to cling to your hand (6).

It looks pretty weird—let everyone get a good look at the cards so that they can appreciate what's happened. Then walk up to someone, saying, "This is the bit that hurts—me, not you." Slowly touch that person on the shoulder. Having watched you generate all that static, he'll be worried about what's going to happen. As soon as you touch him, yell out in pain. Immediately curl the fingers of your right hand and let all

15

the cards fall to the floor. It looks as if you have suddenly discharged all the static electricity that was holding them in place. Shake the last card free, if necessary, shouting, "Ow! Ow! I hate that bit!"

Clutching your right hand as if you've been electrocuted, you'll have plenty of cover to steal away the blob of adhesive with your left hand and then later drop it into your pocket. Hold out your right hand for examination, saying, "Sometimes I get a blister." Fortunately, on this occasion you won't. People will want to examine the cards and try for themselves. It won't be long before someone is shuffling his feet against the carpet trying to build up enough static.

NOTES

Any kind of adhesive can be used for this trick, even chewing gum, which is very easy to get rid of—just pop it back into your mouth as you kiss your imaginary blister better!

TRICK 4

All you need for this trick is a pair of ordinary dice. Whenever anyone adds up the top and bottom numbers of two dice, they get the number 14. Once you understand the principle that makes it work, you'll be able to devise your own presentations.

Start by handing the dice to a spectator. Ask the person to roll them a couple of times so that he is sure they're not loaded, or trick dice. Now take off your watch, telling the spectators you're going to make a prediction. The key number in this routine is 14. That's the number you're going to set on your watch.

If you have a watch with hands, set the minute hand to 1 and the hour hand to 4. If you have a digital watch, set the minute numbers to 13, which gives you a minute to do the rest of the trick before the minute numbers change to 14. Don't reveal your prediction to the spectators yet. Just place your watch face-down on someone's palm and get the person to put his other hand on top so that no one can get at it.

Now turn to the spectator with the dice and say, "This time I want you to roll the dice for real, and we're going to use the top and bottom numbers. OK—roll 'em." When the dice come to a stop, ask the spectator to add up the two top numbers and call out the total. When that's done, ask him to turn one of the dice completely over and add the bottom number. When that is done, ask him to turn over the second die and add that bottom number, too.

As long as the person has followed your instructions, he will always arrive at a total of 14. "Fourteen," you say, "that's strange—take a look at my watch. What numbers are the hands set at?" The spectator should be amazed to find that the hands are set at 1 and 4.

NOTES

This trick works because the top and bottom numbers of all dice always add up to 7. Because we're using two dice, the totals add up to 14. You can make the prediction in many different ways; instead of using your watch, you could just write it down, but the more dramatic you make the revelation, the better.

TRICK 5

O nce you get a reputation as a magician, people will start asking you to teach them a trick. It's difficult to refuse. On the other hand, you don't actually want to start giving your tricks away. This routine is a good compromise—you turn the spectator into the magician.

You choose a card and he finds it. Yet the spectator is completely baffled as to how he did it. Having been pestered to teach a trick, you hand the spectator a deck of cards, saying, "OK, try this—you'll be the magician and I'll be the spectator. Here, take the deck and give it a shuffle."

As he shuffles, offer him a few compliments on his technique. "That's a good technique. I think you're going to be great at this," you say. Then stop him shuffling the cards and tell him it's time you took a card. "I'll take a card and you'll be able to tell me what it is. Sounds good?" Sounds too good to be true! He has no idea how you can make good on this promise.

Get him to hold the cards up toward you and spread them so that you can see the faces. Pretend to be a difficult customer, saying, "Let me try to pick a difficult card. This'll get ya!"

What you're actually doing is spreading through the cards so that you can get a good look at the two top cards of the deck. Let's assume they're the eight of hearts and the king of spades. You'll cross-reference these two cards to lead you to a third card. For instance, if you mix the numbers and suits of the two examples here, you could arrive at either the king of hearts or the eight of spades. Either card will work for this trick, so simply look through the deck until you find either of them and then take it out. Let's assume you take out the eight of spades. Put it face-down on the table, saying, "Perfect. You'll never guess this unless you're really a magician. Let's see."

Tell the spectator to square up the cards again. Remember the two cards you spotted earlier will be on top of the deck. Now ask him to deal cards face-down one at a time into a pile on the table. As he's dealing, you say to him, "Now, a real magician would know exactly when to stop. Do you know when to stop?" He'll probably admit that he has no idea. So just tell him, "Stop dealing any time you like. You're the magician. It's your decision."

Magic

At some point the spectator will stop dealing cards onto the table. Tell him to put the rest of the cards away for the moment. Then ask him to square up the pile on the table and pick it up. "OK, you're nearly there," you say. "Now all you've got to do is deal the cards alternately into two piles." Make sure he follows your instructions properly, dealing one card to the right and then one to the left, and so on, until he has no cards left in his hand. Now, if you've been following this closely, you'll realize that the top cards of the two piles are now the same cards you noted earlier—the eight of hearts and the king of spades.

Here's how you use that information. Ask him to turn over the top card of one of the piles. Let's assume it's the eight of hearts. Now, this is the same value as the card you placed face-down on the table, so ask the spectator, "What value is that card?" He'll say, "Eight." Tell him to turn over the top card of the other pile, the king of spades. This is the same suit as the card you placed on the table, so ask him, "And what suit is that?" He'll answer, "Spades." Point to the eight of hearts and ask him again for its value. Then point to the king of spades and ask him for its suit.

Keep doing this so that he's constantly repeating the words, "Eight, spades, eight, spades." Finally, point to the face-down card you placed on the table and say, "And what card do you think I took earlier?" He'll inevitably say, "Eight of spades." Turn up the card and show that he's correct. Then turn to him and say, "That's the best I've ever seen it done. But please, don't tell anyone how you did it—it's our little secret."

NOTES

The only time this trick won't work is if the two top cards are the same value or suit: for example, a queen of hearts and queen of clubs, or a six of hearts and a nine of hearts. To get around this, just take one of those cards, look at it for a moment, and then push it back into the middle of the deck, saying, "No, that was way too easy. Let me take another one." You can do this as many times as you like. It's all part of the fun of you playing the role of the awkward spectator.

TRICK 6

This is one of the most fundamental and important moves in coin magic. It's called palming and allows you to hide a coin in your hand without anyone being aware of it.

Let's take a look at the secret position the coin will be held in. It's gripped by the muscles at the base of the thumb on one side and the

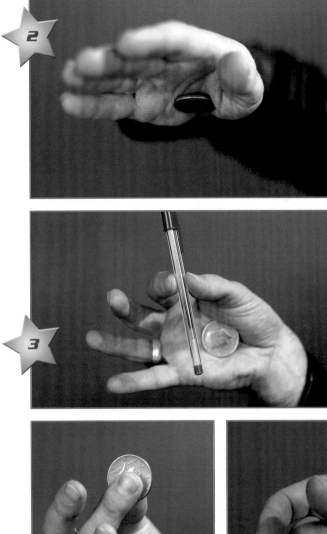

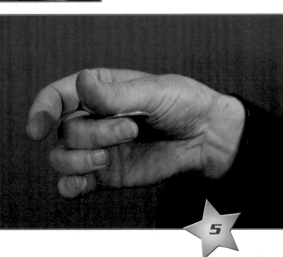

fleshy part of the palm on the other (1). It takes a lot of practice to hold the coin there comfortably, but when it's held properly you can turn the hand completely over and the coin won't fall free (2). Although you have a coin palmed in your hand, you're still able to pick up other objects with your thumb and fingers (3).

You can even wiggle or snap your fingers. Still being able to use the hand for other actions while palming is

what makes it so deceptive. To get the coin into the correct position, start with it on the tips of the right fingers (4). Using the middle finger, push the coin along the underside of the thumb (5).

If you push it far enough, the coin will automatically finish at the correct position for palming (6). Getting the coin from the fingers to the classic palm only takes a second, and it can be performed with the hand casually by your side or in motion. You even can place your hand momentarily in your pocket, pick up a coin from your change and classic-palm it without the action being noticed by the audience.

NOTES

The classic palm is so basic to coin magic that I'd recommend you practice it at every available opportunity. Spend enough time on it and you'll discover that you can palm more than one coin at a time. T. Nelson Downs, an American magician who used to bill himself as "The King of Koins" (great magician, lousy speller!), could palm a dozen or more silver dollars with ease. Now that's dedication.

Time for your first sleight-of-hand coin trick. It uses a move known as the "French Drop," and it can be used to make a coin disappear. It looks as if you take a coin in your left hand and then close your fingers around it. You blow on the hand, open the fingers, and the coin has gone.

Begin by taking a coin out of your pocket and holding it at the tips of the right fingers and thumb (1).

The position of the right hand and the coin is very important. The fingers are below the coin and the thumb on top. The coin is held with the flat side facing the spectators.

As you hold the coin, make some casual comment, such as, "This will work with any coin, but the newer the better—it has to do with the copper content." This is not true, but it gets the spectators intrigued as to what on earth you're going to do. The left hand comes over the coin (2), and the coin is apparently taken away (3). This is where the French Drop takes place, however, because as soon as the

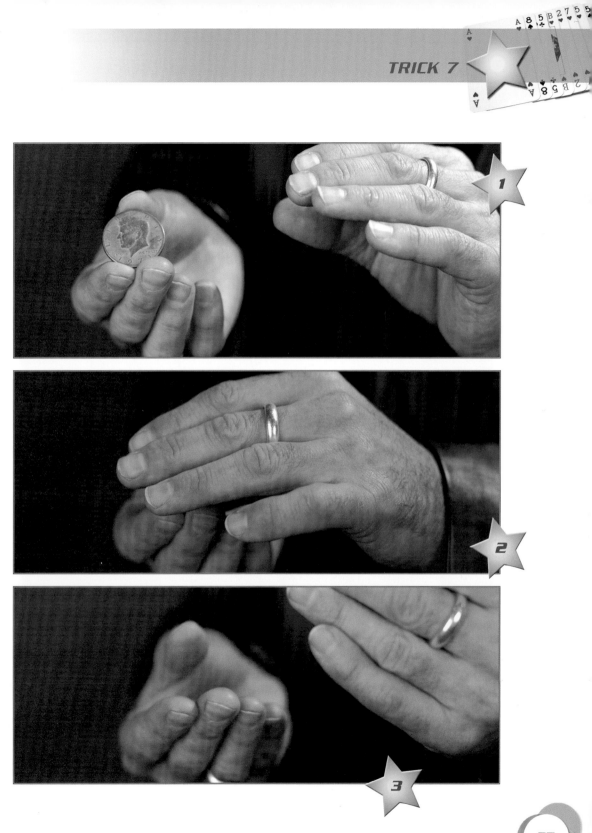

coin was hidden behind the left fingers, it dropped on to the right fingers (4). The photo shows the performer's point of view.

Now close the left fingers and thumb as if actually taking the coin and move the hand away to the left. Spectators will see an empty space between the right fingers and thumb where the coin used to be. In fact, the coin is hidden from their view by the curve of your right fingers (5).

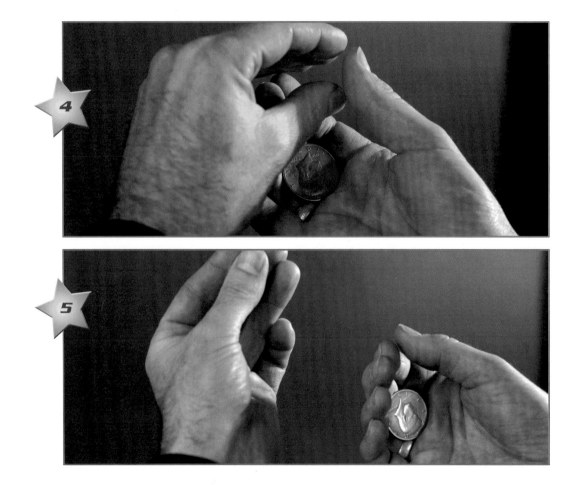

You will find that the coin can be held securely and comfortably in the curled fingers of the right hand. This is known as the "finger palm." Continue moving the left hand to the left, closing it slightly as if it's holding the coin. As you do this, casually let the right hand and its finger-palmed coin fall by your right side.

It's a tried-and-tested rule of magic that wherever you look, the spectators will tend to look. You're able to direct the attention of the spectators to any area you choose while performing tricks, so if you look at the left hand as it moves to the left, the spectators will usually look at that hand, too. By drawing attention to the left hand, you're also drawing attention away from the guilty right hand. Following up your earlier remark about copper content, say, "And the odd thing is that if you apply a little friction to warm it up, like this, something strange happens." Rub the fingers of the left hand together as if applying friction to the coin. At the same time, you classic palm the coin that's in the right hand.

Here's a reminder: as your right hand hangs by your side, let the coin fall to the fingertips. Now with the right middle finger, push the coin upward along the underside of the thumb until it reaches the palm. Keep pushing the coin until it can be held between the thumb muscle on one side and the fleshy part of the palm on the other.

From the spectators' point of view, it doesn't look as if there could be any coin hidden in the right hand. OK, back to the trick. Finish pretending to rub the coin and then extend your left hand. With your right hand, reach up and grasp the left sleeve at the elbow. Pull the sleeve back as you say, "Watch." Squeeze the fingers of your left hand together as if crushing the coin and then open them one by one to reveal that the coin has completely disappeared. The trick is over: the coin has apparently been crushed into nothingness!

However, this does leave you with a coin palmed in the right hand, which is never a good position to be in. Don't be in a hurry to get rid of the evidence, though: as the saying goes, "There's no need to run if no one is chasing you." There's no bigger giveaway than seeing a magician immediately go to his pockets after something has disappeared. Don't be afraid of keeping the coin palmed. As far as the audience is concerned, it's gone and the trick's over.

If you don't act guilty, the spectators will have no reason to assume that you are. Move on to your next trick and ditch the coin in your pocket when the heat is off.

NOTES

The biggest hurdle in this trick is not the mechanics of the French Drop; it's the ability to make the moves smooth and natural. Always keep in mind what you're supposed to be doing—simply taking a coin from the right hand in the left hand prior to making it disappear.

A good tip is to take the coin in the left hand for real several times and study what the movements look like before trying to copy them using the move. If you're wearing a shirt or jacket with a breast pocket, you actually can get rid of the coin completely. When you pull your left sleeve back, allow the right hand to come right over the opening of the breast pocket. You'll find that from this position you can drop the coin from the palm position directly into the breast pocket.

At the end of the trick, both hands are completely empty. Make sure that your pocket is empty at the start of the trick. You don't want to give the game away by someone hearing the coin clink against something inside as it drops.

Another way of getting rid of the need to ditch the palmed coin is to reproduce it. You can use that old standby of pretending to reach out and pluck it from behind a spectator's ear. To do this, you first direct the spectators' attention to someone in the audience by looking at him, saying, "What's that there?"

As you stare at his ear, relax your body, allow your right hand to fall by your side and the coin to fall on to the fingers. Then reach up behind the person's head and as you do, use your thumb to push the coin to the fingertips. As he asks, "What?" you reply, "Here it is!" and pull your hand back as if really pulling the coin from his ear. The better your acting at this point, the better the effect on the audience.

It's an old trick, but it still goes down well, particularly with children. Another comical finish is to produce the coin from your nose. Reach up with the right hand and grasp the bridge of your nose between the right fingers and thumb. The left hand is held palm-up at chest height below the nose. Make a nose-blowing sound and then let the coin fall from the right palm on to the left hand. From the front, it looks exactly as if it's been snorted out of your nose!

TRICK 8

When you've mastered the French Drop, you can progress to this little baffler. You take a coin and tap it with a pen. The coin disappears. You take the cap off the pen and apparently shake the coin out of it. It's a quick magical sequence, which looks absolutely impossible.

Let's assume that the pen is in your breast pocket, where it can be easily reached with your left hand. Borrow a coin and hold it at the right fingertips in position for the French Drop (1). Say, "This coin's very deceptive. Looks solid, but watch this . . ." Apparently take the coin in the left hand, but actually execute the French Drop (2, 3).

Take out the pen with the right hand and use it as a wand to tap the left hand. Open the left hand to show that the coin has disappeared (4). The coin is actually finger-palmed in the right hand. Tell the spectators, "Looks as if the coin has disappeared, but actually—you're not going to believe this—it's inside the pen!" This clearly doesn't

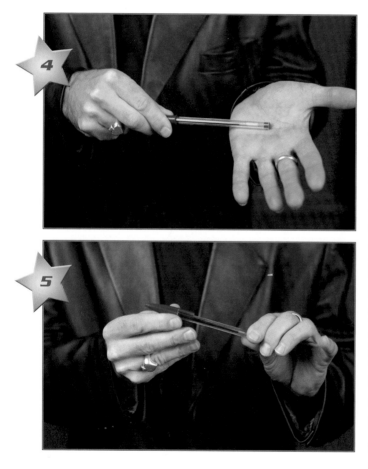

make much sense because there's no way the coin can fit within the diameter of the pen.

Nevertheless, make a play of handling the pen so that the spectators truly believe that your hands are otherwise empty. Reposition the pen so that the right hand can pull the cap off (5). Don't worry: the coin palmed in your right hand will be hidden from the audience. Remove the cap from the pen. Now bring the cap to a vertical position and give it a couple of

sharp shakes as if trying to dislodge something from inside. On the final one, allow the palmed coin to fall from your hand, saying, "There it is!"

Done on the down-swing, it appears as if the coin has suddenly popped out of the pen cap (6): clearly an impossibility. All you need to do now is pocket your pen and hand the coin back to the spectator.

NOTES

Once you understand the handling of the trick, you can choreograph it to suit yourself. The main thing to learn is to be open and easy with the moves. If working over a table, then allow the coin to drop on to it when it reappears. But if you're standing when you perform, you might ask a spectator to hold out his hand before you remove the cap from the pen. Then give it a shake and let the coin fall onto his palm for a surprise finish.

TRICK 9

A large silver coin is folded up inside a square of paper. The coin clearly can be seen through a small hole in the paper packet. It really is there, and yet, with a flick the coin visibly jumps right through the small hole, penetrating the wall of its paper prison. This is a genuinely stunning illusion.

The optical illusion that makes this trick work was discovered by Bob Ostin, a very creative magician from Liverpool. The version described here has been simplified to put it within the abilities of those starting out in magic. You'll need one large silver coin. It doesn't need to be huge, but it needs to be a fairly heavy one for it to work properly. Because of the optical illusion involved in the trick, silver works better than copper. You'll also need a square of paper. It should be at least three times larger than the diameter of the coin on all sides.

Fold it into thirds along its length and breadth until you have nine squares, each of which will comfortably take the coin you're using. Fold the paper into thirds and, with a hole punch, create a small hole right through the folded paper. Alternatively, you could cut a square hole using a craft knife.

When you open the paper, you'll have holes through three of the squares (1). That's all the preparation you need. To perform, hand the coin out for inspection, especially if you're using a coin that isn't in common circulation. Then display the paper. "This coin represents Houdini," you say, "and this paper is his prison." You needn't present the story too seriously. Open the paper and place the coin on the center

square (2). Raise the paper toward the spectators so that they can see the coin through the hole in the middle (3).

Your left thumb is on top of the coin. The right hand now folds the right hand side of the paper over the coin. But as it does, two things happen. The first is that the right fingers cover the hole at the front so that the spectators can't see the coin. The second is that the left thumb pulls the coin to the left (4). The photo shows your viewpoint.

As soon as the right side of the paper is folded, the left thumb pushes the coin back to the right.

The result is that the coin is now above the folded right side of the paper (5). The right thumb now grips the coin as the left hand folds the left side of the paper over it. The top third of the paper is now folded down behind the package, followed by the bottom third of the paper. The result is a small package of paper at the fingertips, inside which is the silver coin (6).

As far as the spectators are concerned, the coin is genuinely trapped within the folded package. They can still see it through the hole in the front. In fact, the coin isn't as secure as they imagine, it can actually slide out of the side on your right. But you don't want to slide the coin free just yet. To do that, you use the illusion Bob Ostin discovered. The left hand grips the upper-left corner of the package between the thumb and forefinger, and the right forefinger is bent backward ready to give the packet a hefty flick (7).

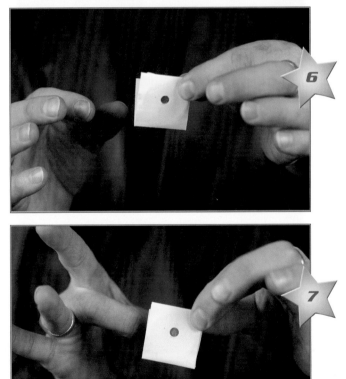

Tell your audience, "They used to say that no prison cell could hold Houdini. He could always escape. Money's got a similar way with me. Watch the coin through the window." Flick the packet. What happens is that the impact shoots the coin out toward the spectators (8).

It actually comes out of the right open side of the packet but so quickly that to the spectators it looks as if the coin has jumped right through the small hole. You'll have to try this in front of a mirror before you can appreciate how effective the illusion is.

NOTES

If you go through the moves slowly, you'll see that the coin is out of the spectators' view for a brief time while you set it in the working position. No one will notice this because you haven't told them to pay attention to the holes in the paper. Only mention them after the coin is set and ready to go. You might want to have the coin signed by a spectator with a marker. That way, when the coin jumps free, they can check that it really is the same coin. As they do that, you can tear up the paper packet to prove that there is only one coin being used. Destroying the paper prevents anyone else from trying the trick for themselves. Sneaky, huh?

TRICK 10

This is a really cool disappearance of a coin. You hold the coin at your fingertips, give it a squeeze, and it completely disappears. Best of all, the method is as clever and straightforward as the effect.

The only drawback to this trick is that you need to be wearing a jacket when you perform it—but then it's about time you've dressed yourself up! The reason you need a jacket is because you're going to shoot the coin up your sleeve. Everyone thinks magicians hide things up their sleeves, and this is one of the few instances when you do! To make it easier, you should roll the sleeves up if you're wearing a long-sleeved shirt. It'll allow the coin an easier passage. Start by borrowing a coin from someone and then holding it up between the thumb and middle finger of your right hand so that everyone can see it (1).

The critical point is that your forearm should be parallel to the floor. In a moment, you're going to flick the coin into the jacket sleeve, and if the forearm is tilted, it will affect the trajectory. Notice, too,

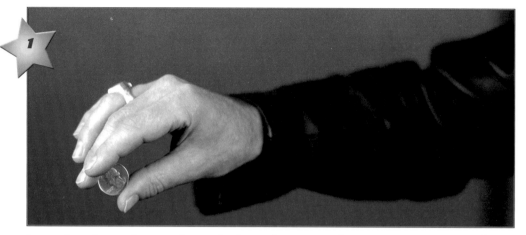

how the sleeve hangs down below the wrist, forming an opening that the coin can enter. A secret tug at the sleeve before you perform this trick will ensure that it hangs loose in the right way.

Draw attention to the coin, saying, "Watch carefully. I'm going to give the coin a squeeze. . ." As you do so, actually squeeze the coin until your thumb and middle finger snap together with the coin flipped into a horizontal position. It will be pinched between the thumb and finger and from the front will be completely hidden (2).

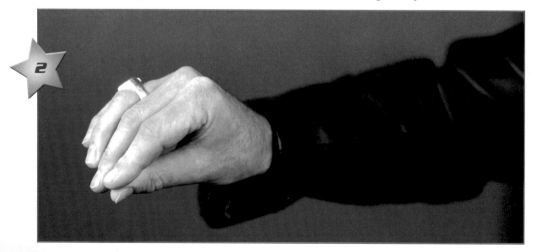

To the audience, it already looks as if the coin has disappeared. In fact, the coin is just projecting behind your closed thumb and fingers (3).

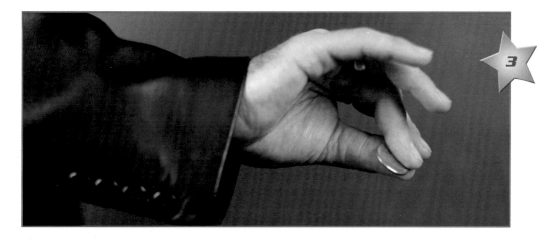

The photo shows a view from the back. Continue, saying, ". . . and it completely disappears." Now snap the middle finger against the thumb. This will result in the coin being flicked back toward the opening of the sleeve (4). These photos show the view from the back.

If you flick it hard enough, it will continue shooting up the sleeve and along the arm. It will stop only when it reaches the elbow. As soon as the coin has gone, open the hand so that the empty palm is toward the spectators (5).

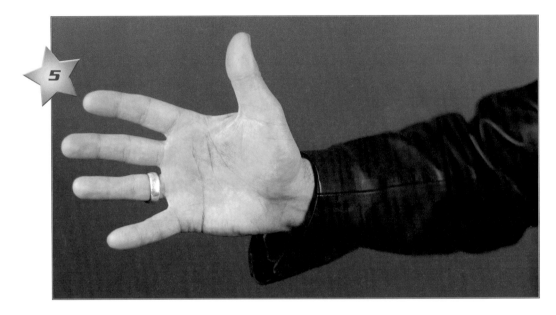

Now they see that the coin really has disappeared. It's an instantaneous disappearance. One moment the coin's there; the next moment it's gone. Turn to the man who loaned you the coin and say, "But the coin hasn't disappeared forever. It's reappeared in your pocket—take a look."

He won't believe this and with good reason—it isn't true. However, as he searches through his pockets, everyone will look at him. If they're looking at him, they won't be looking at you. This gives you a chance to drop your right arm by your side and recover the sleeved coin. The coin will fall down your sleeve and drop into your cupped right fingers.

From here you can classic-palm the coin. By this time, the spectator will be telling you that the coin isn't in his pocket. "I didn't say it would stay there!" you continue. "It carried on over to here." Reach out and produce the coin from behind the next spectator's ear as described earlier in this chapter. "I hope you weren't thinking of keeping that," you say, looking at him suspiciously. "Can't trust anyone these days!"

NOTES

This is probably not a sleight you'll master right away. I recommend you practice with your back to a bed; that way you won't have far to bend every time the coin misses the sleeve! You should make sure that you perform it while wearing the same jacket you rehearsed with. But it'll be worth the time spent because it is very deceptive: it's as close to looking like real magic as you're likely to get.

TRICK 11

You take a large coin and place it on your palm. You brush your other hand across it and instantly it changes into a smaller coin.

This instant and almost visible transformation once again makes use of sleeving. Begin by secretly classic-palming a small coin in your right hand, and then ask the spectators for a large coin. Say, apropos of nothing in particular, "It's amazing how quickly the value of money changes these days." Take the coin from the spectator with your right hand.

The right hand has the coin palmed, but the fact that you're using that hand makes the audience believe both hands are empty at the beginning of this trick. So, take the large coin in the right hand, but be careful not to reveal the palmed smaller one. Drop the large coin on to the palm-up left hand as you talk. The left hand is held just above waist height, which is the perfect position for the change that will follow. The right hand is held palm-down about six inches to the right (1).

This is the starting position for the change. "Take a good look at that coin," you say. Now quickly move the left hand toward you, directly under the palm-down right hand. This will have the effect of propelling the large coin up the right sleeve (2).

At the same time, you move the right hand forward, and as the large coin goes, let the palmed small coin fall on to the left hand. Move the hands apart and let the spectators see that the coin on the left palm has now apparently shrunk, all in the blink of an eye (3).

Hand the coin to the spectator, saying, "Your money's not worth what it used to be, is it?" The change requires a lot of practice and good timing for it to work well.

When you first start to practice, you'll probably exaggerate the movements in order to shoot the coin up the sleeve, but slowly you'll realize that very little movement is required. The hands just come together, the right hand barely covering the left palm for a second. When they separate, the coin has changed.

NOTES

You can retrieve the sleeved coin as your left hand gives the small coin to the spectator. Let the sleeved coin fall into the right hand and classic-palm it. Using the same moves, you can now change the small coin into the large coin—which the spectator will more than likely insist on!

TRICK 12

This is the natural follow-up to the previous trick. You've just transformed a large coin into a small one. You now take the small coin back from the spectator, give it a rub with your fingers and, presto, it's now grown again.

This is simple to do and very magical. The small coin appears to change as the right fingers are rubbed across it. See photos (1), (2), and (3).

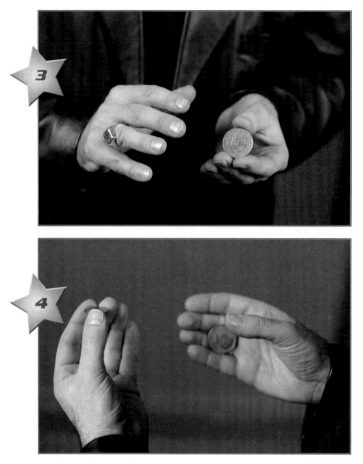

To perform this change, start with the large coin finger-palmed in your right hand. Take the small coin back from the spectator and hold it in your left hand, the "tails" side of the coin facing the spectators. The left thumb is on top of the coin and the fingers below (4). The photo shows an exposed view. The position is very similar to the French Drop position you learned earlier. Say to the spectators, "Did you notice that we started with the coin heads-up last time? Let me show you what happens when it's tails-up." Bring the right hand over the small coin (5).

As soon as the coin is hidden from view, let it fall to the left fingers. The finger-palmed large coin is released so that it can be gripped with the left thumb on top and the left fingers below.

As soon as the exchange of coins has taken place, rub the right fingers on the large coin, saying, "Just warm it up a little and it starts to expand." Move the right hand away entirely, allowing the large coin into view (6). Without making a big deal of it, casually turn your right hand over so that the spectators can see that it's empty. To them, it looks as if you merely rubbed the small coin with your finger-tips and it grew. Hand the coin back, Classic-palm the small coin in your left hand and ditch it at an appropriate moment.

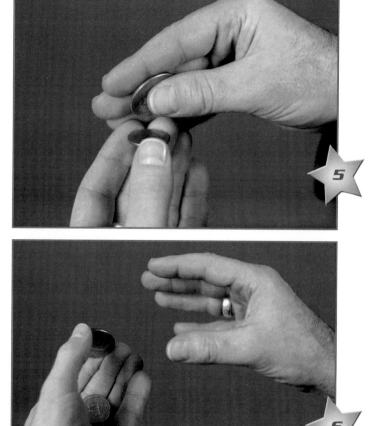

NOTES

You don't have to stop with one coin change. I sometimes have a really big coin in my pocket. Find the most unusual and heaviest coin you can: a Chinese coin or medallion with a hole in it is perfect. As you ditch the small coin, pick up the extra-large coin and just hold it in the finger palm. Ask to see the spectator's coin again. ("Sometimes they come back with a defect.") Position it ready for the move, and this time change the borrowed coin for the whopping hunk of metal that you have finger-palmed. When it's appeared, drop it on the table so that it lands with a clunk. The bigger the coin, the bigger the surprise on the spectators' faces.

TRICK 13

A card is selected, remembered, and returned to the deck. You riffle the end of the deck with a snap and two cards magically turn face-up—the two blackjacks. Unfortunately, neither of them is the selected card. The jacks are replaced in the deck but left face-up, and the deck is cut several times. Finally, the cards are spread out to reveal that the two blackjacks have trapped one card between them. It is, of course, the chosen card.

This uses the key card handling in a slightly different way. Before you perform the trick, you must take out the two blackjacks and place them face-up, at the bottom of the face-down deck. When you bring out the deck, don't reveal the presence of the face-up jacks. Begin by holding the deck face-down in the right hand, and shuffle off some cards into the left hand as you ask a spectator to call out "Stop" any-time they like—the same selection procedure as used in the card trick. Thumb off the top card of the left-hand packet and ask the spectator to look at and remember it before putting it back.

Drop the right-hand packet of cards on top of the selection and square the deck. You can, if you wish, shuffle off a few more cards from the top to the bottom of the deck. Just be careful not to disturb the cards in the middle of the deck, which is where your two face-up jacks now lie. Tell the spectator that you'll snap your fingers and make the selected card turn face-up in the deck. Snap your fingers, but do it twice. Spread the deck between your hands to reveal that there are now two cards face-up in the middle of the deck—the two blackjacks (1). "Oops, sorry," you say, "I should have only done that once—is either of those the card you chose?" They aren't, so you offer to use the black-jacks to find their selection.

Take all the cards that lie above the face-up jacks and put them at the bottom of the deck. Then spread the top few cards so that the jacks can be seen (2). "The blackjacks will find your card: let me show you." Because of your handling earlier, the card immediately below the jacks is the spectator's selection. Square up the cards in the left hand, but as you do, stick your left little finger under the third card from the top so that it keeps a break between the top three cards and the rest of the deck (3).

The photo shows an exposed view from the side. From the spectator's point of view, the break is totally invisible. With your right hand, lift off the top three cards together. The right fingers are at the front of the packet and the thumb at the inner end (4). The left thumb

then peels the top card of this packet back on to the deck and pushes it forward slightly so that it over-hangs at the front. This is known as an "outjog" (5). From the audience's point of view, you are just displaying the

two face-up blackjacks, but in reality you have the spectator's selection hidden under the right-hand jack. Place this jack under the deck so that it sticks out a little at the inner end. This is known as an "injog" (6). Be careful that you don't expose the face-down card hidden below it.

"Two jacks with another fifty cards between them and one of them is yours. Watch the jacks go into action," you say. Square the jacks up so that they're flush with the deck and then give the deck a complete

cut. Hand it to the spectator, inviting him to give the deck a second cut. Make sure he completes the cut, taking a block of cards from the top and placing them on the bottom. Then ask him to give the deck one more cut, "for luck." That's three cuts in total. To the audience, it's the equivalent of mixing up the cards, but as explained in the previous trick, this cutting procedure doesn't alter the sequence of cards. What the cuts have done is brought the two blackjacks together either side of the selected card. Snap your fingers over the deck and then ask the spectator to spread the cards slowly between his hands. He'll find your two blackjacks face-up in the center, but now there's a single face-down card between them (7).

Reach into the spread and take out this three-card sandwich. Ask him to name his chosen card, then turn the three cards over to reveal that they've succeeded in finding his selection.

NOTES

If the spectator looks a bit clumsy with his handling of the cards, then take the deck back from him and spread it out yourself. Do it slowly and openly—you don't want anyone thinking that you're doing anything sneaky at this stage. If you master the ribbon spread, you can use that to make a flashier finish.

GLOSSARY

choreograph To organize or arrange a combination of movements.

classic-palm To hide a coin in one's palm, holding it without the aid of fingers.

finger-palm To hold a coin in one's curled fingers so that it's hidden from view.

French Drop A magician's technique of dropping a coin without opening the palm so that the audience doesn't know that it has ever left the hand.

improvisation To act without planning.

intuition One's gut feeling or sudden insight.

misdirection A magician's tool that trains the viewers' eyes away from what the magician doesn't want them to see.

palming Similar to the classic-palm, palming is holding a coin with the base of the thumb and the palm so that it is not seen.

sleeving Hiding a coin or other object in one's sleeve.

spectators People who are watching a performance; audience.

spontaneity Acting without forethought or planning.

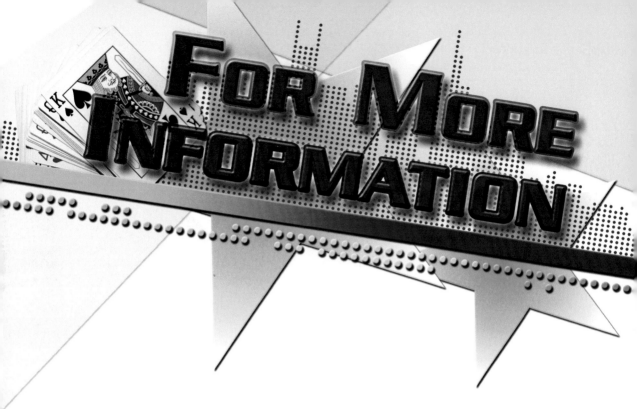

The Magic Castle
Academy of Magical Arts
7001 Franklin Avenue
Hollywood, CA 90028-8600
(323) 851-3313
Web site: http://www.magiccastle.com

The Magic Depot!
7914 East 40th Street
Tulsa, Oklahoma 74145
(918) 641-0707
Web site: http://www.magic.org

Magic Times
Meir Yedid Magic
P.O. Box 2566
Fair Lawn, NJ 07410

(201) 703-1171
Web site: http://www.magictimes.com
E-mail: meir@mymagic.com

Magic Tricks, Inc.
2768 Columbia Road
Gordonsville, VA 22942
(540) 832-0900
Web site: http://www.magictricks.com

Web Sites

Due to the changing nature of Internet links, Rosen Publishing has
developed an online list of Web sites related to the subject of this book.
This site is updated regularly. Please use this link to access the list:

http://www.rosenlinks.com/am/ssha

Angel, Criss. *Mindfreak: Secret Revelations*. New York, NY: HarperEntertainment, 2007.

Becker, Herbert L. *101 Greatest Magic Secrets Exposed*. New York, NY: Citadel, 2002.

Copperfield, David. *David Copperfield's Beyond Imagination*. New York, NY: HarperCollins Publishers, 1997.

Hugard, Jean. *The Royal Road to Card Magic*. Mineola, NY: Dover Publications, 1999.

Johnson, Karl. *The Magician and the Cardsharp: The Search for America's Greatest Sleight-of-Hand Artist*. New York, NY: Henry Holt and Co., 2005.

Kalush, William. *The Secret Life of Houdini: The Making of America's First Superhero*. New York, NY: Atria, 2006.

Lemezma, Marc. *Mind Magic: Extraordinary Tricks to Mystify, Baffle and Entertain*. London, England: New Holland, 2005.

Rourke, Dennis. *The Everything Card Tricks Book: Over 100 Amazing Tricks to Impress Your Friends and Family!* Avon, MA: Adams Media Corporation, 2005.

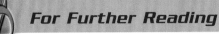

Scarne, John. *Scarne on Card Tricks*. Mineola, NY: Dover Publications, 2003.

Schiffman, Nathaniel. *Abracadabra!: Secret Methods Magicians & Others Use to Deceive Their Audience*. Amherst, NY: Prometheus Books, 1997.

Steinmeyer, Jim. *The Magic of Alan Wakeling: The Works of a Master Magician*. New York, NY: Carroll & Graf, 2006.

Sumpter, Gary. *Ultimate Street Magic: Amazing Tricks for the Urban Magician*. London, England: New Holland Publishers, 2006.

Wilson, Mark. *Mark Wilson's Complete Course in Magic*. Philadelphia, PA: Running Press 2003.

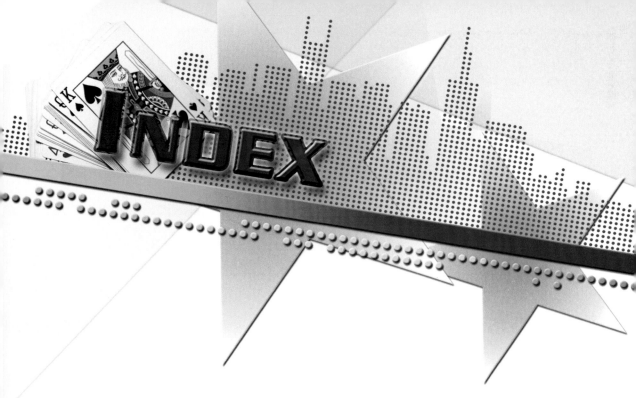

INDEX

SIMPLE SLEIGHT-OF-HAND:
Card and Coin Tricks for the Beginning Magician

About the Author

Paul Zenon has dozens of TV credits to his name, including his own shows *Paul Zenon's Trick or Treat*, *Paul Zenon's Tricky Christmas*, and *White Magic with Paul Zenon*. He has also appeared on many other television shows, including *History of Magic*, *Secret History—Magic at War*, *The World's 50 Greatest Magic Tricks*, and many more. Zenon has performed in around thirty countries and in every conceivable location, from the Tropicana Hotel in Las Vegas to the hold of an aircraft carrier in the Adriatic; from the London Palladium to a clearing in the jungles of Belize; from the Magic Castle in Hollywood to the back of a truck in the Bosnian war zone.

Designers: Interior, Nelson Sá; Cover, Tahara Anderson
Editor: Nicholas Croce
Photography: Karl Adamson